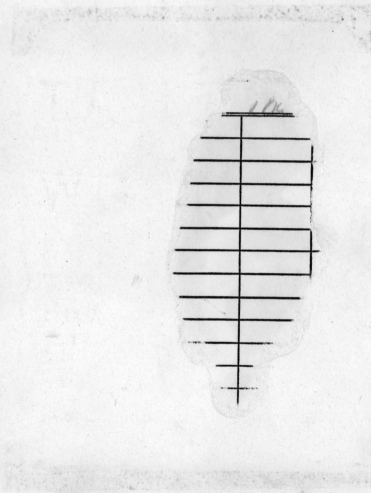

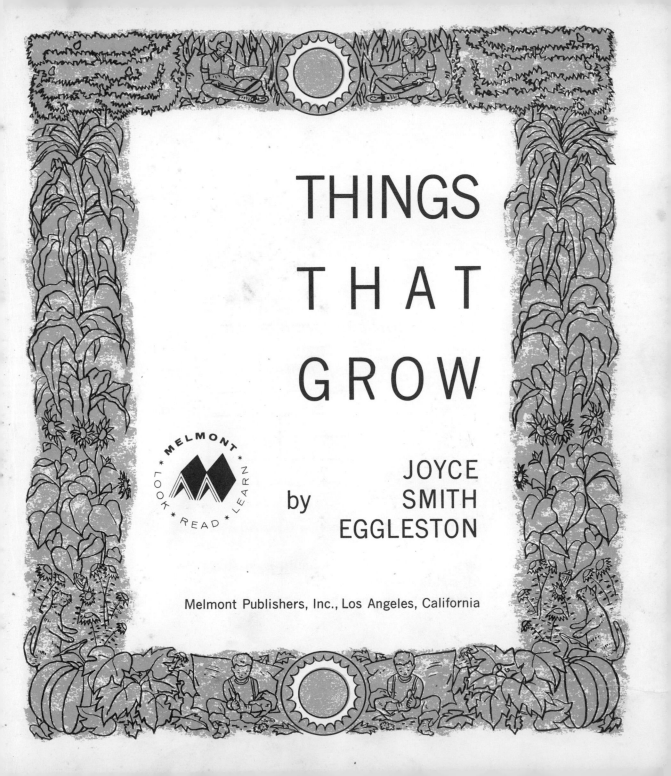

THINGS

THAT

GROW

MELMONT
★ LOOK ★ READ ★ LEARN ★

by **JOYCE
SMITH
EGGLESTON**

Melmont Publishers, Inc., Los Angeles, California

To Laura and Ernie Smith,

my mother and dad.

Library of Congress Catalog Card Number 58-9989

THINGS

THAT

GROW

Girls and boys grow.

Animals grow.
Plants grow, too.

Things that grow need: sunlight,
air,
water,
food,
and rest.

To grow, girls need sunlight.

To grow, boys need sunlight.

To grow, animals need sunlight.

To grow, plants need sunlight, too.

To grow, girls need air.

To grow, boys need air.

To grow, animals need air.

To grow, plants need air, too.

To grow, girls need water.

To grow, boys need water.

To grow, animals need water.

To grow, plants need water, too.

To grow, girls need food.

To grow, boys need food.

To grow, animals need food.

To grow, plants need food, too.

To grow, girls need rest.

To grow, boys need rest.

To grow, animals need rest.

To grow, plants need rest, too.

Things that grow need: sunlight,
air,
water,
food,
and rest.

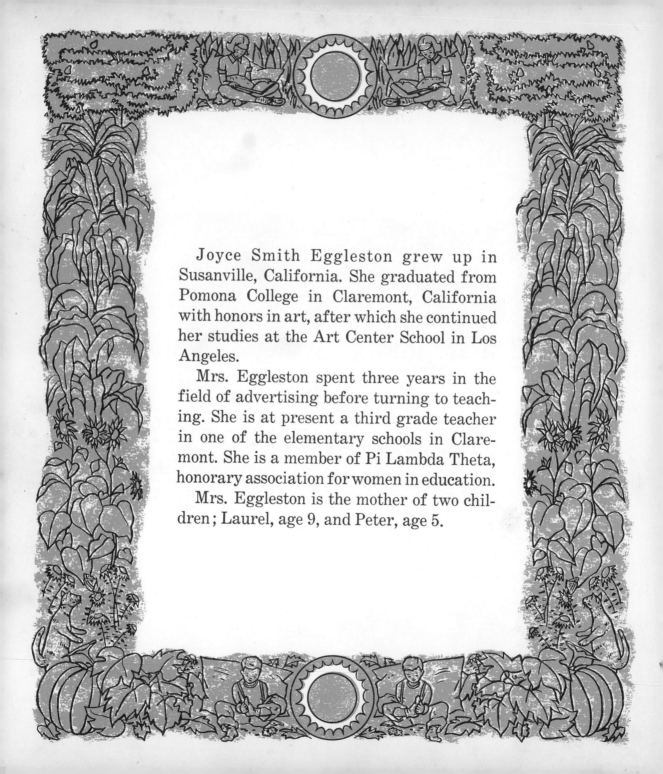

Joyce Smith Eggleston grew up in Susanville, California. She graduated from Pomona College in Claremont, California with honors in art, after which she continued her studies at the Art Center School in Los Angeles.

Mrs. Eggleston spent three years in the field of advertising before turning to teaching. She is at present a third grade teacher in one of the elementary schools in Claremont. She is a member of Pi Lambda Theta, honorary association for women in education.

Mrs. Eggleston is the mother of two children; Laurel, age 9, and Peter, age 5.